OXFORD REVISE

EDEXCEL GCSE

HISTORY

Anglo-Saxon and Norman England, c1060–88

COMPLETE REVISION AND PRACTICE

Series Editor: Aaron Wilkes

Aaron Wilkes

OXFORD
UNIVERSITY PRESS

Contents

Shade in each level of the circle as you feel more confident and ready for your exam.

How to use this book iv

1 Anglo-Saxon society in c1060 2
- Knowledge
- Retrieval
- Practice

2 Edward the Confessor and the succession crisis 6
- Knowledge
- Retrieval
- Practice

3 The Norman invasion 12
- Knowledge
- Retrieval
- Practice

4 Establishing control 16
- Knowledge
- Retrieval
- Practice

5 Anglo-Saxon resistance 20
- Knowledge
- Retrieval
- Practice

6 The feudal system and the Church 26
- Knowledge
- Retrieval
- Practice

7 Norman government 32
- Knowledge
- Retrieval
- Practice

8 The Norman aristocracy 36
- Knowledge
- Retrieval
- Practice

9 William I and his sons 40
- Knowledge
- Retrieval
- Practice

How to use this book

This book uses a three-step approach to revision: **Knowledge**, **Retrieval**, and **Practice**. It is important that you do all three; they work together to make your revision effective.

Knowledge

Knowledge comes first. Each chapter starts with a **Knowledge Organiser**. These are clear easy-to-understand, concise summaries of the content that you need to know for your exam. The information is organised to show how one idea flows into the next so you can learn how everything is tied together, rather than lots of disconnected facts.

Answers and Glossary

You can scan the QR code at any time to access the sample answers and mark schemes for all the exam-style questions, glossary containing definitions of the key terms, as well as further revision support. go.oup.com/OR/GCSE/Ed/Hist/AngloSax

REVISION TIP

Revision tips offer you helpful advice and guidance to aid your revision and help you to understand key concepts and remember them.

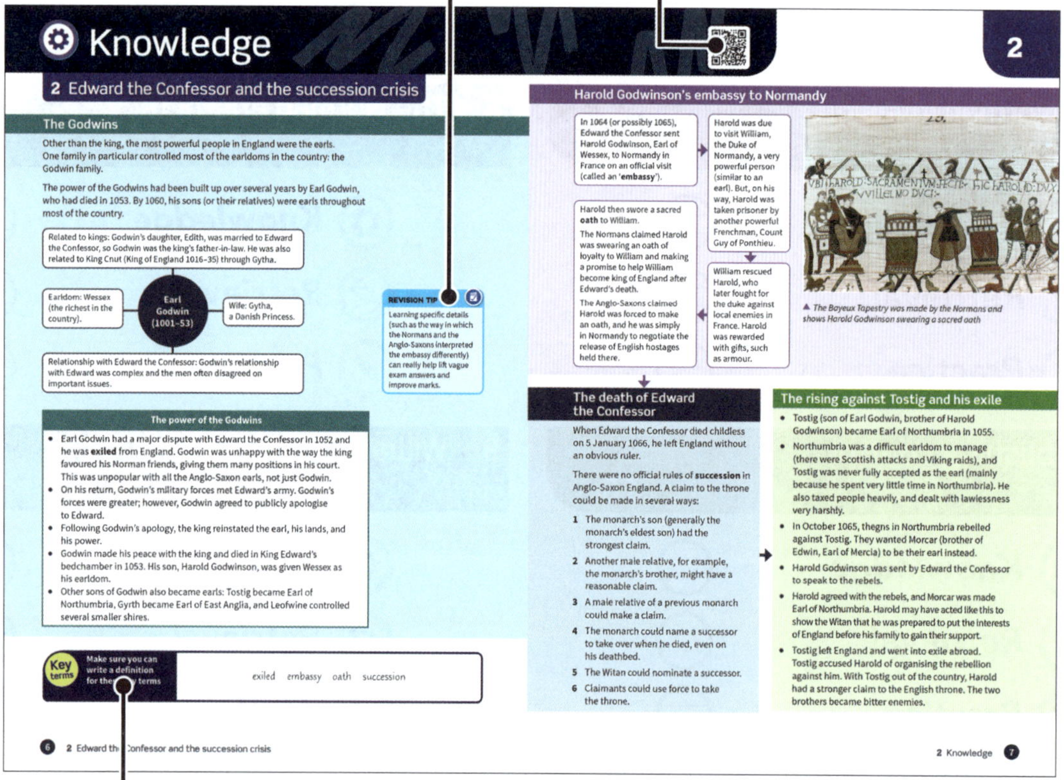

Knowledge

2 Edward the Confessor and the succession crisis

The Godwins

Other than the king, the most powerful people in England were the earls. One family in particular controlled most of the earldoms in the country: the Godwin family.

The power of the Godwins had been built up over several years by Earl Godwin, who had died in 1053. By 1060, his sons (or their relatives) were earls throughout most of the country.

Related to kings: Godwin's daughter, Edith, was married to Edward the Confessor, so Godwin was the king's father-in-law. He was also related to King Cnut (King of England 1016–35) through Gytha.

Earldom: Wessex (the richest in the country).

Earl Godwin (1001–53)

Wife: Gytha, a Danish Princess.

Relationship with Edward the Confessor: Godwin's relationship with Edward was complex and the men often disagreed on important issues.

REVISION TIP

Learning specific details (such as the way in which the Normans and the Anglo-Saxons interpreted the embassy differently) can really help lift vague exam answers and improve marks.

The power of the Godwins

- Earl Godwin had a major dispute with Edward the Confessor in 1052 and he was **exiled** from England. Godwin was unhappy with the way the king favoured his Norman friends, giving them many positions in his court. This was unpopular with all the Anglo-Saxon earls, not just Godwin.
- On his return, Godwin's military forces met Edward's army. Godwin's forces were greater; however, Godwin agreed to publicly apologise to Edward.
- Following Godwin's apology, the king reinstated the earl, his lands, and his power.
- Godwin made his peace with the king and died in King Edward's bedchamber in 1053. His son, Harold Godwinson, was given Wessex as his earldom.
- Other sons of Godwin also became earls: Tostig became Earl of Northumbria, Gyrth became Earl of East Anglia, and Leofwine controlled several smaller shires.

Key terms — Make sure you can write a definition for these key terms: exiled, embassy, oath, succession

6 2 Edward the Confessor and the succession crisis

2

Harold Godwinson's embassy to Normandy

In 1064 (or possibly 1065), Edward the Confessor sent Harold Godwinson, Earl of Wessex, to Normandy in France on an official visit (called an '**embassy**').

Harold was due to visit William, the Duke of Normandy, a very powerful person (similar to an earl). But, on his way, Harold was taken prisoner by another powerful Frenchman, Count Guy of Ponthieu.

William rescued Harold, who later fought for the duke against local enemies in France. Harold was rewarded with gifts, such as armour.

Harold then swore a sacred **oath** to William.

The Normans claimed Harold was swearing an oath of loyalty to William and making a promise to help William become king of England after Edward's death.

The Anglo-Saxons claimed Harold was forced to make an oath, and he was simply in Normandy to negotiate the release of English hostages held there.

▲ The Bayeux Tapestry was made by the Normans and shows Harold Godwinson swearing a sacred oath

The death of Edward the Confessor

When Edward the Confessor died childless on 5 January 1066, he left England without an obvious ruler.

There were no official rules of **succession** in Anglo-Saxon England. A claim to the throne could be made in several ways:

1 The monarch's son (generally the monarch's eldest son) had the strongest claim.
2 Another male relative, for example, the monarch's brother, might have a reasonable claim.
3 A male relative of a previous monarch could make a claim.
4 The monarch could name a successor to take over when he died, even on his deathbed.
5 The Witan could nominate a successor.
6 Claimants could use force to take the throne.

The rising against Tostig and his exile

- Tostig (son of Earl Godwin, brother of Harold Godwinson) became Earl of Northumbria in 1055.
- Northumbria was a difficult earldom to manage (there were Scottish attacks and Viking raids), and Tostig was never fully accepted as the earl (mainly because he spent very little time in Northumbria). He also taxed people heavily, and dealt with lawlessness very harshly.
- In October 1065, thegns in Northumbria rebelled against Tostig. They wanted Morcar (brother of Edwin, Earl of Mercia) to be their earl instead.
- Harold Godwinson was sent by Edward the Confessor to speak to the rebels.
- Harold agreed with the rebels, and Morcar was made Earl of Northumbria. Harold may have acted like this to show the Witan that he was prepared to put the interests of England before his family to gain their support.
- Tostig left England and went into exile abroad. Tostig accused Harold of organising the rebellion against him. With Tostig out of the country, Harold had a stronger claim to the English throne. The two brothers became bitter enemies.

2 Knowledge 7

Key terms — Make sure you can write a definition for these key terms

The **Key terms** box highlights the key words and phrases you need to know, remember and be able to use confidently.

Retrieval

The **Retrieval questions** help you learn and quickly recall the information you've acquired. These are short questions and answers about the content in the Knowledge Organiser you have just reviewed. Cover up the answers with some paper and write down as many answers as you can from memory. Check back to the Knowledge Organiser for any you got wrong, then cover the answers and attempt all the questions again until you can answer *all* the questions correctly.

Make sure you revisit the Retrieval questions on different days to help them stick in your memory. You need to write down the answers each time, or say them out loud, otherwise it won't work.

Previous questions

Each chapter also has some **Retrieval questions** from **previous chapters**. Answer these to see if you can remember the content from the earlier chapters. If you get the answers wrong, go back and do the Retrieval questions for the earlier chapters again.

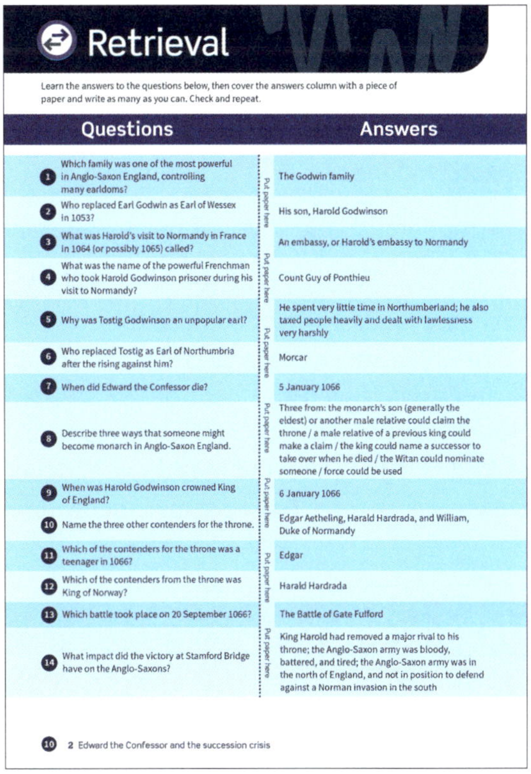

Retrieval

Learn the answers to the questions below, then cover the answers column with a piece of paper and write as many as you can. Check and repeat.

Questions	Answers
1 Which family was one of the most powerful in Anglo-Saxon England, controlling many earldoms?	The Godwin family
2 Who replaced Earl Godwin as Earl of Wessex in 1053?	His son, Harold Godwinson
3 What was Harold's visit to Normandy in France in 1064 (or possibly 1065) called?	An embassy, or Harold's embassy to Normandy
4 What was the name of the powerful Frenchman who took Harold Godwinson prisoner during his visit to Normandy?	Count Guy of Ponthieu
5 Why was Tostig Godwinson an unpopular earl?	He spent very little time in Northumberland; he also taxed people heavily and dealt with lawlessness very harshly
6 Who replaced Tostig as Earl of Northumbria after the rising against him?	Morcar
7 When did Edward the Confessor die?	5 January 1066
8 Describe three ways that someone might become monarch in Anglo-Saxon England.	Three from: the monarch's son (generally the eldest) or another male relative could claim the throne / a male relative of a previous king could make a claim / the king could name a successor to take over when he died / the Witan could nominate someone / force could be used
9 When was Harold Godwinson crowned King of England?	6 January 1066
10 Name the three other contenders for the throne.	Edgar Aetheling, Harald Hardrada, and William, Duke of Normandy
11 Which of the contenders for the throne was a teenager in 1066?	Edgar
12 Which of the contenders from the throne was King of Norway?	Harald Hardrada
13 Which battle took place on 20 September 1066?	The Battle of Gate Fulford
14 What impact did the victory at Stamford Bridge have on the Anglo-Saxons?	King Harold had removed a major rival to his throne; the Anglo-Saxon army was bloody, battered, and tired; the Anglo-Saxon army was in the north of England, and not in position to defend against a Norman invasion in the south

10 2 Edward the Confessor and the succession crisis

Practice

Once you think you know the Knowledge Organiser and Retrieval answers really well, you can move on to the final stage: **Practice**.

Each chapter has **exam-style questions**, including some questions from previous chapters, to help you apply all the knowledge you have learnt and can retrieve.

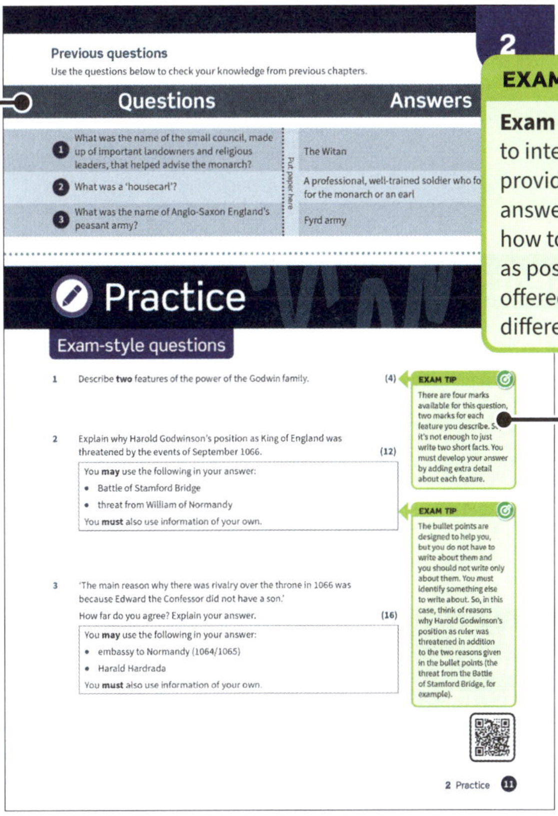

2

Previous questions

Use the questions below to check your knowledge from previous chapters.

Questions	Answers
1 What was the name of the small council, made up of important landowners and religious leaders, that helped advise the monarch?	The Witan
2 What was a 'housecarl'?	A professional, well-trained soldier who fo[...] for the monarch or an earl
3 What was the name of Anglo-Saxon England's peasant army?	Fyrd army

Practice

Exam-style questions

1 Describe **two** features of the power of the Godwin family. (4)

2 Explain why Harold Godwinson's position as King of England was threatened by the events of September 1066. (12)

You **may** use the following in your answer:
- Battle of Stamford Bridge
- threat from William of Normandy

You **must** also use information of your own.

3 'The main reason why there was rivalry over the throne in 1066 was because Edward the Confessor did not have a son.'

How far do you agree? Explain your answer. (16)

You **may** use the following in your answer:
- embassy to Normandy (1064/1065)
- Harald Hardrada

You **must** also use information of your own.

EXAM TIP: There are four marks available for this question, two marks for each feature you describe. S[...] it's not enough to just write two short facts. You must develop your answer by adding extra detail about each feature.

EXAM TIP: The bullet points are designed to help you, but you do not have to write about them and you should not write only about them. You must identify something else to write about. So, in this case, think of reasons why Harold Godwinson's position as ruler was threatened in addition to the two reasons given in the bullet points (the threat from the Battle of Stamford Bridge, for example).

2 Practice 11

EXAM TIP

Exam tips show you how to interpret the questions, provide guidance on how to answer them, and advice on how to secure as many marks as possible. Guidance is also offered on how to approach different command words.

Knowledge

1 Anglo-Saxon society in c1060

The power of the monarch

In 1060, Anglo-Saxon England was a sophisticated and civilised society with around two million inhabitants.

The monarch was the most powerful person in Anglo-Saxon England.

The monarch made laws, set taxes, gave land to loyal followers (and took it away), controlled the **minting** and distribution of coins, and could raise an army if the country was threatened by attack.

Before 1060, much of England had been controlled by Vikings from Scandinavia (which includes Norway, Sweden, and Denmark). Many people who lived there were descendants of Vikings. The monarch still ruled these areas, but the people had their own laws and customs and were allowed some independence.

The monarch in 1060: Edward the Confessor

- Ruled since 1042. His reign had been stable and largely peaceful.
- A respected law-maker, and very religious.
- Married to Edith, the daughter of Earl Godwin (a rich and powerful earl).
- Had no children to inherit the throne after him, and argued a lot with Earl Godwin.

Helping the king

The main earldoms by the 1060s

- The king was helped by **earls**. Each earl controlled an **earldom**. By the 1060s, there were four main earldoms: Wessex, Mercia, Northumbria, and East Anglia.
- The earls advised the king and made sure the king's laws were enforced. They were responsible for the **shires** and the **hundreds**.
- The **Witan** was a small council that also advised the king. It was made up of important landowners and religious leaders such as archbishops and bishops. It discussed threats and land disputes and had a large role in choosing a new monarch.

Local government: the shires and the hundreds

- Earldoms were divided into shires. There were around 40 shires in total.
- A **shire reeve** (sheriff) was responsible for each shire. They collected taxes and fines, held courts to deal with major crimes, and raised an army if needed.
- Shires were divided into hundreds. A hundred contained around 12 villages. Each hundred had its own 'reeve' who held courts to deal with minor crimes.

Key terms **Make sure you can write a definition for these key terms**

minting earls earldom shires hundreds Witan shire reeve diocese treasury thegns housecarls fyrd army tithings wergild burh

The influence of the Church

Religion was important: almost everyone was Christian and accepted what the Church said as absolute fact. The Church was rich, powerful, and organised, with the Archbishops of Canterbury and York at the top.

- The archbishops managed about 15 bishops, each in charge of their own **diocese**.
- The bishops made sure the village priests carried out their duties properly.
- Monks and nuns lived in abbeys, priories, monasteries, and convents. They farmed the land, but also kept records, wrote histories, and looked after the very poor.

Defence

There were two parts to the army.

Army

Housecarls
2 500–3 000 well-trained, professional soldiers who protected the king and earls.

Fyrd army
Peasants, whom the earls and thegns could call upon to fight.

The economy and social system

England was wealthy, and had strong trade links, notably with France and Scandinavia.

England had a developed and effective economic system, with its own minting system for making coins and a **treasury** that coordinated government taxation and spending.

There was a clear hierarchy in Anglo-Saxon society. However, society was flexible: **thegns** could be promoted to earls, for example.

- The monarch
- **Earls:** the richest and most powerful nobles
- **Thegns ('thanes'):** local lords who lived in manor houses. They carried out local duties and had to provide local men for the army when needed.
- **Ceorls ('curls'):** sometimes called 'freemen'. They could work for another lord if they wanted to, but still had to do some work for the local lord as well, including fighting.
- **Peasants:** made up most of the population (around 70 per cent). They farmed land they had rented, but also worked for the local lord for up to three days a week. Male peasants between the ages of 15 and 60 could be asked to fight in the fyrd.
- **Enslaved people:** made up about ten per cent of the population and were viewed more as property than people. Owning enslaved people was a common part of Anglo-Saxon life.

The legal system

- Justice was based on collective responsibility. **Tithings** consisted of around ten households. If a tithing member broke the law, the others had to bring them to court or be punished.
- There was no police force. If a crime was committed, the victim and/or witnesses had to raise the 'hue and cry'. They had to shout loudly so people would come to help catch the criminal.
- Punishments tended to be brutal, with execution and mutilation relatively common.
- The ordeal system was a type of trial. Ordeal by fire or water was used to test the accused's guilt. It was believed that God would save the innocent.
- Blood feuds were common: if someone was killed, the victim's family had the right to kill a member of the murderer's family.
- **Wergild** was a system that aimed to replace blood feuds. Compensation was paid instead of taking revenge for death or injury.

Towns and villages

- Most of England was covered in forest. There were villages and towns where land was farmed.
- Every shire had a fortified town (a **burh**) for administration and trading. Burhs were difficult to attack. Around ten per cent of the population lived in burhs.

Retrieval

Learn the answers to the questions below, then cover the answers column with a piece of paper and write as many as you can. Check and repeat.

Questions	Answers
1 What was the name of England's king in 1060?	Edward the Confessor
2 How was the King of England in 1060 connected to Earl Godwin?	Edward the Confessor was married to Edith, the daughter of Earl Godwin; Godwin was also one of the king's rich and powerful earls
3 What was the name of the small council, made up of important landowners and religious leaders, that helped advise the monarch?	The Witan
4 Which two archbishops were the leading churchmen in Anglo-Saxon England?	The Archbishops of Canterbury and York
5 List the responsibilities of a shire reeve.	Collected taxes and fines; held courts to deal with major crimes; helped raise an army if needed
6 In Anglo-Saxon society, what was the name given to local lords below the earls in the hierarchy?	Thegns
7 What was a 'housecarl'?	A professional, well-trained soldier who fought for the monarch or an earl
8 What was the name of Anglo-Saxon England's peasant army?	Fyrd army
9 How was a 'tithing' used to help keep law and order?	A tithing was a group of around ten households and, if a member of a tithing broke the law, the others had to bring them to court, or be punished; it helped to keep law and order through collective responsibility
10 What was the 'hue and cry'?	A system for trying to catch criminals: you had to shout loudly if you were the victim of, or a witness to, a crime, and people would come to help you catch the criminal
11 What was the 'wergild system'?	A system that meant that compensation was paid instead of taking revenge when someone was killed or injured
12 What was a 'burh'?	A fortified town: every shire had a burh for administration and trading
13 Approximately what percentage of the population lived in a burh?	Ten per cent

Put paper here

Practice

Exam-style questions

1 Describe **two** features of Anglo-Saxon society. **(4)**

EXAM TIP

A 'feature' is something that is distinctive or characteristic. The 'Describe two features...' question always asks you to write about just two features of something, so don't include any more because writing extra features will not get you any more marks.

2 Explain why Anglo-Saxon earls were important in Anglo-Saxon England. **(12)**

You **may** use the following in your answer:

- earldoms
- local government

You **must** also use information of your own.

EXAM TIP

Before attempting to answer each question, use the 'BUG' method:

- **Box the command word**, so that you know what you are being asked to do.
- **Underline the key words** (the words that tell you which topic the question is about, and jog your memory about the topic).
- **Glance at the question again**, to pick up any additional information it is giving you and to help you picture what you need to do.

3 'Control of land was the main reason why Anglo-Saxon monarchs had so much power.'

How far do you agree? Explain your answer. **(16)**

You **may** use the following in your answer:

- earls
- law-making

You **must** also use information of your own.

EXAM TIP

For longer questions always plan your answer. Jot down a few points to give a shape to your answer.

As part of your revision, practise planning answers to questions.

Knowledge

2 Edward the Confessor and the succession crisis

The Godwins

Other than the king, the most powerful people in England were the earls. One family in particular controlled most of the earldoms in the country: the Godwin family.

The power of the Godwins had been built up over several years by Earl Godwin, who had died in 1053. By 1060, his sons (or their relatives) were earls throughout most of the country.

Related to kings: Godwin's daughter, Edith, was married to Edward the Confessor, so Godwin was the king's father-in-law. He was also related to King Cnut (King of England 1016–35) through Gytha.

Earl Godwin (1001–53)

Earldom: Wessex (the richest in the country).

Wife: Gytha, a Danish Princess.

Relationship with Edward the Confessor: Godwin's relationship with Edward was complex and the men often disagreed on important issues.

REVISION TIP

Learning specific details (such as the way in which the Normans and the Anglo-Saxons interpreted the embassy differently) can really help lift vague exam answers and improve marks.

The power of the Godwins

- Earl Godwin had a major dispute with Edward the Confessor in 1052 and he was **exiled** from England. Godwin was unhappy with the way the king favoured his Norman friends, giving them many positions in his court. This was unpopular with all the Anglo-Saxon earls, not just Godwin.
- On his return, Godwin's military forces met Edward's army. Godwin's forces were greater; however, Godwin agreed to publicly apologise to Edward.
- Following Godwin's apology, the king reinstated the earl, his lands, and his power.
- Godwin made his peace with the king and died in King Edward's bedchamber in 1053. His son, Harold Godwinson, was given Wessex as his earldom.
- Other sons of Godwin also became earls: Tostig became Earl of Northumbria, Gyrth became Earl of East Anglia, and Leofwine controlled several smaller shires.

Key terms Make sure you can write a definition for these key terms

exiled embassy oath succession

Harold Godwinson's embassy to Normandy

In 1064 (or possibly 1065), Edward the Confessor sent Harold Godwinson, Earl of Wessex, to Normandy in France on an official visit (called an '**embassy**').

Harold was due to visit William, the Duke of Normandy, a very powerful person (similar to an earl). But, on his way, Harold was taken prisoner by another powerful Frenchman, Count Guy of Ponthieu.

William rescued Harold, who later fought for the duke against local enemies in France. Harold was rewarded with gifts, such as armour.

Harold then swore a sacred **oath** to William.

The Normans claimed Harold was swearing an oath of loyalty to William and making a promise to help William become king of England after Edward's death.

The Anglo-Saxons claimed Harold was forced to make an oath, and he was simply in Normandy to negotiate the release of English hostages held there.

▲ *The Bayeux Tapestry was made by the Normans and shows Harold Godwinson swearing a sacred oath*

The death of Edward the Confessor

When Edward the Confessor died childless on 5 January 1066, he left England without an obvious ruler.

There were no official rules of **succession** in Anglo-Saxon England. A claim to the throne could be made in several ways:

1. The monarch's son (generally the monarch's eldest son) had the strongest claim.
2. Another male relative, for example, the monarch's brother, might have a reasonable claim.
3. A male relative of a previous monarch could make a claim.
4. The monarch could name a successor to take over when he died, even on his deathbed.
5. The Witan could nominate a successor.
6. Claimants could use force to take the throne.

The rising against Tostig and his exile

- Tostig (son of Earl Godwin, brother of Harold Godwinson) became Earl of Northumbria in 1055.
- Northumbria was a difficult earldom to manage (there were Scottish attacks and Viking raids), and Tostig was never fully accepted as the earl (mainly because he spent very little time in Northumbria). He also taxed people heavily, and dealt with lawlessness very harshly.
- In October 1065, thegns in Northumbria rebelled against Tostig. They wanted Morcar (brother of Edwin, Earl of Mercia) to be their earl instead.
- Harold Godwinson was sent by Edward the Confessor to speak to the rebels.
- Harold agreed with the rebels, and Morcar was made Earl of Northumbria. Harold may have acted like this to show the Witan that he was prepared to put the interests of England before his family to gain their support.
- Tostig left England and went into exile abroad. Tostig accused Harold of organising the rebellion against him. With Tostig out of the country, Harold had a stronger claim to the English throne. The two brothers became bitter enemies.

Knowledge

2 Edward the Confessor and the succession crisis

The coronation and reign of Harold Godwinson

Following the death of his father, Earl Godwin, Harold Godwinson became an extremely important figure in Edward the Confessor's government. He was *sub-regulus*, acting as 'deputy king', from 1060 onwards. He was also Edward's brother-in-law and had shown his loyalty, even over his own brother Tostig.

Harold claimed that Edward had promised him the throne on his deathbed. He had the support of the English nobles and the Witan (who were gathered near Harold in London, making it easier for him to get their support). Harold had himself crowned king on 6 January 1066, the same day as Edward's funeral.

After his coronation, Harold visited the important northern city of York to make sure he had the support of powerful people there. In May, he mobilised a fleet of ships and a fyrd army in the south to guard the coast against any attempted invasion by William, Duke of Normandy.

Rivals for the throne

There were three other strong claimants to the throne.

Edgar Aetheling (c1051–1126)	Harald Hardrada (1015–66)	William, Duke of Normandy (c1028–87)
• Great-nephew of Edward the Confessor (a blood relation). • Lived with Edward since childhood and treated as Edward's adopted son. • Had the support of many English earls because he was an Anglo-Saxon. • Was a teenager in 1066, so lacked the experience, and political and military skill, to challenge Harold's coronation.	• Viking King of Norway, with a reputation as a strong and powerful warrior. • Because Edward the Confessor had no sons, he believed that another relative of the king should take over. He was related to King Cnut, who had ruled England from 1016–35. • Claimed his father, Magnus, had been promised the throne by Cnut's son Harthacnut. When Harthacnut died in 1042, Edward took the throne. Magnus had since died, but his son was determined to claim what he thought was rightfully his.	• Duke of Normandy since the age of seven. • Successful but ruthless military leader. • Distant cousin of Edward the Confessor, through Edward's mother, Emma of Normandy. Some suggest there was a friendship between William and Edward, although they only met a few times. • Claimed Edward had promised him the throne when William had visited England several years before. • Edward grew up in Normandy and the way he ruled was clearly influenced by this. Some historians have argued Edward's actions as king suggest he wanted a Norman to succeed him. • Claimed Harold Godwinson had sworn to support William's claim to the throne in 1064. William claimed the oath had been made over a holy relic and was therefore binding in the eyes of God.

William prepares to invade and Hardrada invades

After Harold's coronation, William prepared to invade England, but the invasion was delayed for six weeks due to bad weather.

Meanwhile, King Harold had been forced to send the fyrd army home. Most were farmers, and it was harvest time, so they were needed back in the fields.

Harald Hardrada made his move. Hardrada and 300 Viking ships sailed up the River Humber and landed 16 km from the city of York.

King Harold's supporters in the north of England were ready to defend their land, and the first battle of 1066 began.

The Battle of Gate Fulford (20 September 1066)

Events and outcome

- Hardrada and around 7 000 Vikings were joined by Tostig (King Harold's brother).
- The Anglo-Saxons were commanded by King Harold's brothers-in-law, Edwin (Earl of Mercia) and Morcar (Earl of Northumbria). The army had around 3 500 men.
- The initial Anglo-Saxon attack took the Vikings by surprise but Viking numbers overwhelmed the Anglo-Saxon army and Edwin and Morcar were defeated. Hardrada was victorious.

Significance

- The Anglo-Saxon army was scattered and the earls were forced to flee. Thousands of English soldiers were killed or wounded, so fewer were available to fight against an invasion by William.
- However, the Vikings suffered significant casualties too.

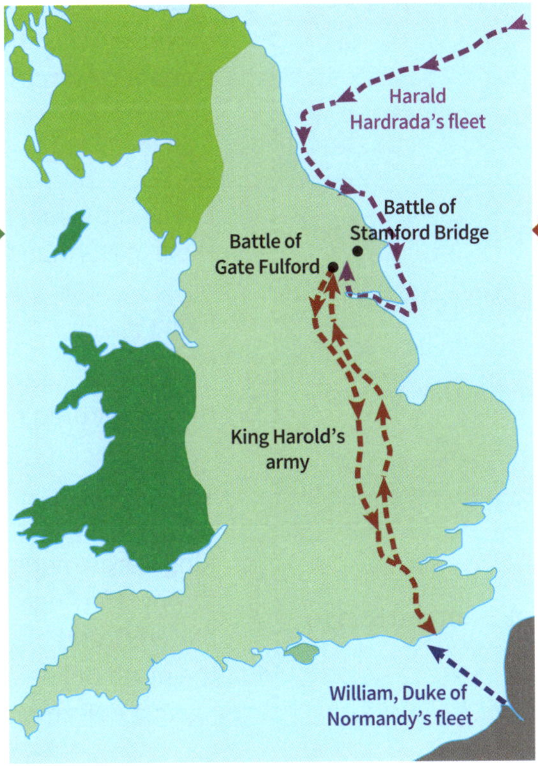

The Battle of Stamford Bridge (25 September 1066)

Events and outcome

- The loss at Gate Fulford meant that King Harold had to move quickly. He assembled an army and marched 306 km north from London in four days, gathering more troops as he went.
- The Anglo-Saxons reached Tadcaster, on the outskirts of York, on 24 September and, the following morning, they launched a surprise attack on the Viking camp.
- The battle was centred around the undefended Stamford Bridge and was long and bloody. The Vikings were scattered and not ready for battle but still fought hard. However, Hardrada and Tostig were both killed.

Significance

- King Harold had destroyed the Viking threat and removed a rival to the throne.
- Harold's victory was a great one, but the Anglo-Saxon army was now bloody, battered, and tired.
- Three days later, word reached Harold that William's fleet had finally landed in the south. Harold now had to return south.

Retrieval

Learn the answers to the questions below, then cover the answers column with a piece of paper and write as many as you can. Check and repeat.

Questions		Answers
1	Which family was one of the most powerful in Anglo-Saxon England, controlling many earldoms?	The Godwin family
2	Who replaced Earl Godwin as Earl of Wessex in 1053?	His son, Harold Godwinson
3	What was Harold's visit to Normandy in France in 1064 (or possibly 1065) called?	An embassy, or Harold's embassy to Normandy
4	What was the name of the powerful Frenchman who took Harold Godwinson prisoner during his visit to Normandy?	Count Guy of Ponthieu
5	Why was Tostig Godwinson an unpopular earl?	He spent very little time in Northumberland; he also taxed people heavily and dealt with lawlessness very harshly
6	Who replaced Tostig as Earl of Northumbria after the rising against him?	Morcar
7	When did Edward the Confessor die?	5 January 1066
8	Describe three ways that someone might become monarch in Anglo-Saxon England.	Three from: the monarch's son (generally the eldest) or another male relative could claim the throne / a male relative of a previous king could make a claim / the king could name a successor to take over when he died / the Witan could nominate someone / force could be used
9	When was Harold Godwinson crowned King of England?	6 January 1066
10	Name the three other contenders for the throne.	Edgar Aetheling, Harald Hardrada, and William, Duke of Normandy
11	Which of the contenders for the throne was a teenager in 1066?	Edgar
12	Which of the contenders from the throne was King of Norway?	Harald Hardrada
13	Which battle took place on 20 September 1066?	The Battle of Gate Fulford
14	What impact did the victory at Stamford Bridge have on the Anglo-Saxons?	King Harold had removed a major rival to his throne; the Anglo-Saxon army was bloody, battered, and tired; the Anglo-Saxon army was in the north of England, and not in position to defend against a Norman invasion in the south

Put paper here

Previous questions

Use the questions below to check your knowledge from previous chapters.

	Questions	Answers
1	What was the name of the small council, made up of important landowners and religious leaders, that helped advise the monarch?	The Witan
2	What was a 'housecarl'?	A professional, well-trained soldier who fought for the monarch or an earl
3	What was the name of Anglo-Saxon England's peasant army?	Fyrd army

Put paper here

Practice

Exam-style questions

1 Describe **two** features of the power of the Godwin family. **(4)**

EXAM TIP

There are four marks available for this question, two marks for each feature you describe. So, it's not enough to just write two short facts. You must develop your answer by adding extra detail about each feature.

2 Explain why Harold Godwinson's position as King of England was threatened by the events of September 1066. **(12)**

You **may** use the following in your answer:

- Battle of Stamford Bridge
- threat from William of Normandy

You **must** also use information of your own.

EXAM TIP

The bullet points are designed to help you, but you do not have to write about them and you should not write only about them. You must identify something else to write about. So, in this case, think of reasons why Harold Godwinson's position as ruler was threatened in addition to the two reasons given in the bullet points (the threat from the Battle of Stamford Bridge, for example).

3 'The main reason why there was rivalry over the throne in 1066 was because Edward the Confessor did not have a son.'

How far do you agree? Explain your answer. **(16)**

You **may** use the following in your answer:

- embassy to Normandy (1064/1065)
- Harald Hardrada

You **must** also use information of your own.

Knowledge

3 The Norman invasion

The build-up to the Battle of Hastings

- **11 August** – Duke William is ready to launch an invasion from Normandy, but bad weather prevents this.
- **28 September** – William lands at Pevensey; King Harold marches south after victory over Vikings at Stamford Bridge on 25 September.
- **6 October** – King Harold and the remnants of his army reach London.
- **11 October** – King Harold leaves London, choosing not to wait for 30 000 reinforcements, and marches to meet William.
- **13 October** – King Harold reaches the South Downs, near Hastings, where William's forces are.

REVISION TIP

Knowing the order of events (chronology) helps make sense of things. Here, for example, knowing that Harold was in another part of England when William landed, helps you to understand some of the reasons why he lost at Hastings.

English and Norman troops and tactics

The table below gives a comparison of the two armies' resources, tactics, and leadership at Hastings.

	King Harold and the Anglo-Saxons	Duke William and the Normans
Troops	• Around 7 000 on foot. • Mostly poorly trained fyrd, with some thegns, and elite housecarls. • Survivors of the fight against the Vikings were exhausted, having marched 300 km (190 miles) south following Harold's decision to head straight into battle.	• Around 7 000 trained soldiers. Infantry including highly skilled archers, and cavalry (soldiers on horseback). • Were well rested, having landed several days before.
Weaponry and armour	• Double-handed axes, pikes, large circular shields. • Housecarls had armour; peasants used farming equipment plus weapons and armour taken from fallen soldiers.	• Bows, pikes, large tear-shaped shields that covered from chin to knee. • Infantry and cavalry wore armour.
Battle tactics and strategy	• Positioned on the top of Senlac Hill. It is easier to fight downhill. • Army was behind a shield wall (interlocking shields to prevent an enemy advance). Shield walls are a very effective defence tactic, but it is difficult to attack in this formation.	• Positioned at the bottom of Senlac Hill, with marshy land either side. It is harder to fight uphill. • Army was organised into divisions and a flag system was used for communication so tactics could be changed during battle.
The leaders	• Harold was an experienced general: had successfully fought the Welsh and the Vikings. • Had many supporters in England, including most nobles and the Witan. • On foot throughout the battle.	• William was a highly experienced general: had conquered areas around Normandy and also Sicily. • Had the support of the Pope, the king of France, and the leaders of states bordering Normandy. • On horseback throughout the battle.

Key events of the Battle of Hastings

Battle begins

The battle began at 9 a.m. on 14 October 1066. The Anglo-Saxons formed their shield wall, and the Normans were unable to break through. Norman arrows flew over the heads of the English frontline or hit the shields. Charging uphill, the cavalry proved useless against the firm Anglo-Saxon line.

Rumour of William's death

At one point, it was rumoured that William had been killed, but he rode among his troops and tipped his helmet back to show he was alive.

First feigned retreat

After a number of failed attacks, one group of Normans ran back from the line. Sensing victory, a group of Anglo-Saxons gave chase, causing a break in the shield wall. When they became trapped in the marshland, the Anglo-Saxons were slaughtered. William ordered more **feigned retreats** like this and finally the Anglo-Saxon line began to be worn down.

Archers moved forward

During a break in the battle to allow both sides to recover their dead and wounded, William changed tactics. He moved his archers to the front and ordered them to fire into the air. The arrows landed on top of the Anglo-Saxons, behind the shield wall, causing chaos.

Final push

Fearing the arrival of Anglo-Saxon reinforcements, William made one final push for victory. A combination of the feigned retreats, constant arrow fire, and a full-scale cavalry attack meant that by late afternoon the Anglo-Saxon shield wall had almost disintegrated.

Harold killed

As their shield wall fell, the Anglo-Saxons were cut to pieces by the advancing Normans. At some point during this part of the battle, King Harold was killed. With their leader dead and the battle lost, many Anglo-Saxons began to drift away. William had won.

Reasons for William's victory

- The Normans were well organised with clear communication around the battlefield. William could be seen by his men because he fought on horseback, unlike Harold who was on foot with his men.
- William's men believed God was on their side – they were fighting under the **Papal Banner**.
- William had archers and cavalry – Harold did not. This gave William additional weaponry, and greater manoeuvrability.
- William chose the battle site, so had time to organise his troops properly and make preparations. Harold's men were unrested and depleted after fighting at Stamford Bridge.
- Hardrada had invaded at the same time as William, forcing Harold to fight at two ends of the country. This gave William's army time to rest before the battle.
- The weather delayed William's invasion over the summer. This meant that Harold had to send the fyrd army in the south home so they could harvest their crops.

Key terms Make sure you can write a definition for these key terms

feigned retreat   Papal Banner

Retrieval

Learn the answers to the questions below, then cover the answers column with a piece of paper and write as many as you can. Check and repeat.

	Questions	Answers
1	On what date did King Harold win the Battle of Stamford Bridge?	25 September 1066
2	When did Duke William land in England?	28 September 1066
3	Approximately how many soldiers made up the Anglo-Saxon army?	Around 7000
4	Duke William's army consisted of which three types of soldier?	Infantry, cavalry, and archers
5	Define 'cavalry'.	Soldiers on horseback
6	Why was Harold's army already tired when the Battle of Hastings began?	Harold and the survivors of the fight against the Vikings marched straight to battle against William after winning the Battle of Stamford Bridge
7	Which leader positioned their troops on the top of Senlac Hill before the battle?	King Harold
8	What was a 'shield wall'?	Interlocking shields to prevent an enemy advance
9	List an advantage and a disadvantage to a shield wall.	Advantage: hard to break so was a very effective defence Disadvantage: it was difficult to attack using this formation
10	On what date was the Battle of Hastings?	14 October 1066
11	At approximately what time did the battle begin?	9 a.m.
12	At one point, it was rumoured that William had been killed. How did William react?	He rode among his troops and tipped his helmet back to show he was alive
13	What was a 'feigned retreat'?	A tactic where soldiers from one side pretend to retreat in the hope that enemy soldiers will follow and be in a vulnerable position
14	Why did William's men believe they had God on their side?	They were fighting under the Papal Banner
15	Harold fought on foot. List one advantage and one disadvantage of this for Harold.	Advantage: Harold showed his men he was willing to fight alongside them Disadvantage: Harold's ability to move around easily and communicate with his troops was limited
16	Who won the Battle of Hastings?	William, Duke of Normandy

Put paper here

Previous questions

Use the questions below to check your knowledge from previous chapters.

	Questions	Answers
1	What was a 'burh'?	A fortified town: every shire had a burh for administration and trading
2	When was Harold Godwinson crowned King of England?	6 January 1066
3	What impact did the victory at Stamford Bridge have on the Anglo-Saxons?	King Harold had removed a major rival to his throne; the Anglo-Saxon army was bloody, battered, and tired; the Anglo-Saxon army was in the north of England, and not in position to defend against a Norman invasion in the south

Put paper here

Practice

Exam-style questions

1 Describe **two** features of the Anglo-Saxon army at the Battle of Hastings. **(4)**

2 Explain why there was a succession crisis when Edward the Confessor died. **(12)**

> You **may** use the following in your answer:
> - Edward dies without an obvious successor
> - embassy to Normandy (1064/1065)
>
> You **must** also use information of your own.

3 'The main reason for the Anglo-Saxon defeat at the Battle of Hastings was superior Norman tactics.'

How far do you agree? Explain your answer. **(16)**

> You **may** use the following in your answer:
> - feigned retreats
> - fyrd army
>
> You **must** also use information of your own.

EXAM TIP

Get into the habit of quickly identifying the focus of the question. This is a question you need to answer quickly (five minutes). In this case, you should be immediately thinking of Harold's army.

EXAM TIP

Remember that you are being asked 'how far' you agree with the quote. So, to what extent you think that William's superior tactics played a part in the Anglo-Saxon defeat.

Don't just write about feigned retreats and the fyrd army. You can mention these, of course, but you must primarily think about Norman tactics and the role they played in the Norman victory. Was it primarily these tactics that led to victory, or did other things play a role – and to what extent?

Knowledge

4 Establishing control

William's next steps

Despite victory at Hastings, William still had much to do to achieve control of England. Anglo-Saxon earls Edwin and Morcar had not been at Hastings, and there were still significant English forces in London ready to oppose him.

1 Moved east to Kent to secure the trading ports used by the Anglo-Saxons and to allow supplies to be brought in from Normandy.

2 Strengthened his hold on land he had captured by building motte and bailey castles as he moved towards London.

3 Secured control of Canterbury, the centre of the English Church.

4 Burnt Southwark in retaliation for London's refusal to submit to him.

5 Secured Winchester, the base of the English **treasury**.

6 Ordered the burning of land between Berkhamsted and London, depriving the area of supplies and giving him complete control over it.

7 Meeting was held at Berkhamsted where William received an **oath of fealty** from Edgar (Edward the Confessor's great nephew), earls Edwin and Morcar, bishops, and leading men of London.

8 By the time he was crowned on Christmas Day 1066, William had enough power to claim to be the King of England.

▲ *William's progress to his coronation*

William I and the Anglo-Saxons

William I remained concerned about Anglo-Saxon rebellion, so tried not to provoke an attack. He:

- ☑ promised to rule by the same laws as Edward the Confessor
- ☑ allowed Edwin and Morcar to keep their lands
- ☑ retained England's leading archbishops, Stigand, and Aldred
- ☑ promised Anglo-Saxon thegns who had not fought at Hastings that they could buy back land.

Rewarding followers

William I rewarded the people who had supported his invasion:

- ☑ Land taken from Anglo-Saxons who had fought at Hastings was given to William's loyal Norman supporters.
- ☑ Rich gifts were sent to the Pope and to those who had fought with him at Hastings.

The problem of the Marches

The Marches are the border area between England and Wales. To solve the potential threat of powerful Welsh princes in the Marches, William created three new earldoms (the Marcher earldoms) and appointed loyal Normans as the new earls.

This gave William security in the Marches:

- The new earls had great power and total control over the court system, taxes, and building in their earldoms.
- They did not have to pay heavy taxes to William, so could spend money building many castles and creating new towns to dominate their earldoms.

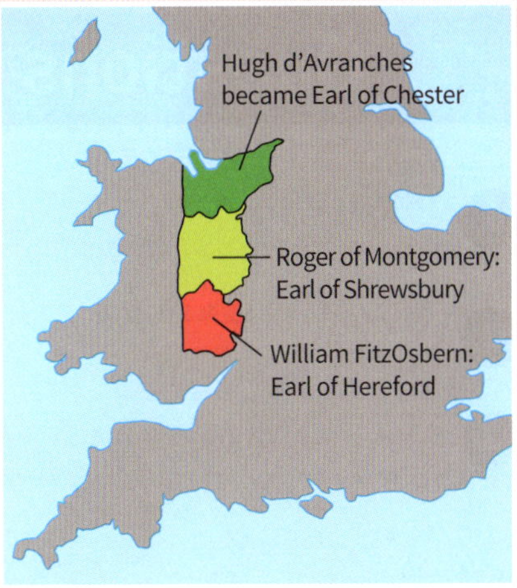

▶ *The Marcher earldoms*

The Normans build castles

The first castles built by the Normans were wooden structures known as **motte and bailey castles**. They could be built in a matter of weeks, often using the natural features of the landscape.

By 1070, wood had been replaced by stone for most new castles. By 1086, around 48 large castles and many other smaller ones had been built in England.

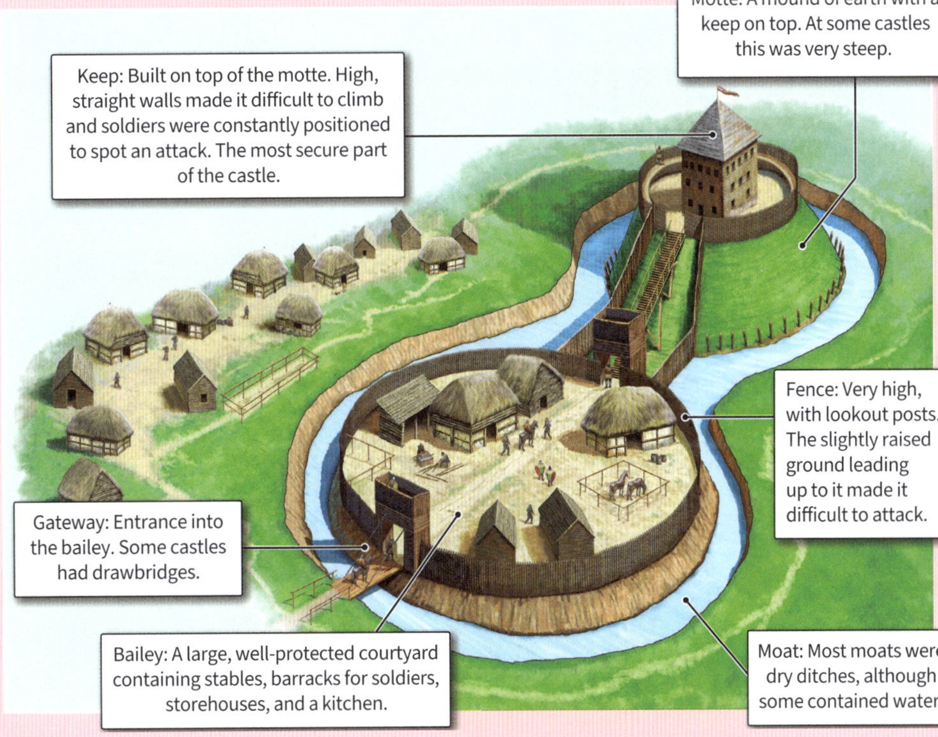

Castles were important for several reasons. They:

- acted as a centre of administration for an area
- protected Norman settlers, particularly the new lords
- intimidated the local population and showed power
- established control of an area
- demonstrated the social structure of Norman England – the Norman rulers lived in castles on the top of hills and their Anglo-Saxon subjects lived at the bottom.

Key terms **Make sure you can write a definition for these key terms**

oath of fealty   treasury   the Marches   motte and bailey castles

Retrieval

Learn the answers to the questions below, then cover the answers column with a piece of paper and write down as many as you can. Check and repeat.

	Questions	Answers
1	Which two powerful Anglo-Saxon earls had not been at the Battle of Hastings?	Edwin and Morcar
2	Why did William secure the trading ports in Kent?	To stop Anglo-Saxon trade and allow supplies to be brought in from Normandy
3	When was William crowned King of England?	Christmas Day 1066
4	Give two examples of things William I did so as not to provoke an Anglo-Saxon rebellion.	Two from: he promised to rule by the same laws as Edward the Confessor / allowed Edwin and Morcar to keep their lands / retained England's leading archbishops (Stigand and Aldred) / promised Anglo-Saxon thegns who had not fought at Hastings that they could buy back land
5	How did William I reward his followers?	Land taken from Anglo-Saxons who had fought at Hastings was given to William's loyal Norman supporters. Also, William sent rich gifts to both the Pope and others who had fought alongside him at Hastings
6	Where were the Marches?	The border area between England and Wales
7	Why was William I so keen to control the Marches?	Because of the potential threat from powerful Welsh princes
8	Name the three new Marcher earldoms.	Chester, Shrewsbury, and Hereford
9	What was a 'motte'?	A mound of earth with a keep on top. At some castles this was very steep
10	What was a 'bailey'?	A large, well-protected courtyard containing stables, barracks for soldiers, storehouses, and a kitchen
11	What was the highest part of a motte and bailey castle?	The keep
12	List two ways that castles helped the Normans control England.	Two from: they acted as a centre of administration for an area / they protected Norman lords and settlers / they intimidated the local population and showed power / they established control of an area / they were a clear way of demonstrating the social structure of Norman England

Put paper here

Previous questions

Use the questions below to check your knowledge from previous chapters.

Questions	Answers
1 List the responsibilities of a shire reeve.	Collected taxes and fines; held courts to deal with major crimes; helped raise an army if needed
2 Which of the contenders for the throne was a teenager in 1066?	Edgar
3 On what date did King Harold win the Battle of Stamford Bridge?	25 September 1066

Put paper here

Practice

Exam-style questions

1 Describe **two** features of motte and bailey castles. **(4)**

EXAM TIP

You are asked to describe two features – so only describe two! If you cannot think of any relevant details to support one of your features, choose a different feature to write about.

2 Explain why motte and bailey castles were built throughout England after 1066. **(12)**

> You **may** use the following in your answer:
> - the Marcher earldoms
> - Anglo-Saxon rebellion
>
> You **must** also use information of your own.

3 'The main reason William of Normandy won the battle of Hastings was his superior leadership skill.'

How far do you agree? Explain your answer. **(16)**

> You **may** use the following in your answer:
> - Norman tactics
> - Battle of Stamford Bridge
>
> You **must** also use information of your own.

EXAM TIP

This question will always begin with a statement. It will start with phrases such as 'The main reason for…' or 'The main consequence of…'. It's important that you show your thinking about how far you agree with the statement – do you think other reasons or consequences were more important?

5 Anglo-Saxon resistance

King William now had two realms to control: England and Normandy. In the early years of his reign, revolts against Norman rule broke out in different parts of England.

The revolt of earls Edwin and Morcar in 1068

1067

King William feels England is secure enough for him to return to Normandy. He takes Edgar (the great-nephew of Edward the Confessor), and earls Edwin and Morcar with him.

→ Whilst he is away, Edric the Wild starts a revolt with a large number of Anglo-Saxon followers and the support of the Welsh princes. However, the rebellion fails to take hold.

1068

Edgar and earls Edwin and Morcar flee from William's court in Normandy. They gather an army together in the midlands and the north of England, which includes support from Welsh princes.

← William acts quickly. He comes over from Normandy and leads an army northward, building castles and allowing his soldiers to destroy crops and housing on the way.

← Edwin and Morcar surrender without fighting taking place. They are pardoned and return to William's court. Edgar flees to Scotland to the court of King Malcolm III.

Cause of the revolt

- William had not kept a promise he had made to Edwin that he could marry one of his daughters.
- Edwin's earldom and Morcar's earldom had been reduced in size.
- William had imposed heavy taxes, and had taken lots of Anglo-Saxon treasure back to Normandy.
- Norman castles were appearing all over the country, dominating the landscape. Sometimes Anglo-Saxon houses were knocked down to make way for them.

Edgar Aethling and the rebellions in the north (1069)

The north of England was the most rebellious area, as it saw itself as semi-independent from the rest of the country. There was also a large number of people who still had some loyalty to the Vikings.

- After fleeing the rebellions of 1068, Edgar Aethling ('Aethling' means prince) had escaped to Scotland and formed a powerful alliance with King Malcolm III.
- Edgar made a claim on William's throne. Malcolm, who had recently married Edgar's sister, gave his support to the claim.
- Events in the north spiralled out of control in January 1069 when the Norman earl, Robert de Comines, and his men were murdered by Anglo-Saxon rebels. In addition, the Bishop of Durham's house was set on fire and Edgar attacked the city of York.
- To make matters worse, in the summer of 1069, Danish Vikings (led by King Swegn) arrived in 240 ships and joined up with an Anglo-Saxon army led by Edgar and other Anglo-Saxon earls. The joint army defeated the Norman forces outside the castle in York and captured the castle itself.

How did William deal with the rebellions in the north?

Solution 1

William raced north with a large army. As he approached, the Vikings returned to their ships. William paid them money to leave, which they accepted. The Anglo-Saxon army scattered. (When people were taxed to raise money to 'pay off' Viking invaders, it was called a **geld tax**.)

Solution 2

Determined to teach the people of the north a lesson, William began a campaign to destroy vast areas of land around Yorkshire, burning and salting the fields, and killing people and livestock. The event became known as the **Harrying of the North**.

Hereward the Wake and rebellion at Ely (1070–71)

The rebellion of Hereward the Wake in the early 1070s is one of the best-known rebellions of the Norman period.

- Hereward's father was believed to be Leofric, Earl of Mercia. Hereward was angry that William and the Normans had confiscated land from his father and killed his brother.
- With the support of King Swegn of Denmark and Morcar (Edwin had been killed), Hereward began a campaign of **guerrilla**-style attacks on Norman settlers in the marshes and fenlands of East Anglia. His men fought in small groups and hid to take the enemy by surprise.
- Hereward's supporters were able to use their knowledge of the land to avoid capture and frustrate William's attempts to end the rebellion.
- Their best-known attack was the looting and burning of Peterborough Abbey in 1070.
- The rebels were based at the abbey on the Isle of Ely, which was well defended and surrounded by marshland.
- William once again paid King Swegn to leave England, and turned his attention to Morcar and Hereward. Unable to attack directly, he besieged the Isle of Ely and made several attempts to cross the marshland.
- Eventually, William succeeded. Morcar was captured (and imprisoned). Hereward escaped.

The Harrying of the North

After the rebellions in the north in 1069, William wanted to teach the people of the north a lesson. What happened became known as the Harrying of the North.

Reasons

- William was angry that the Anglo-Saxon leaders would not accept him as king.
- In revenge for the deaths of Norman supporters (e.g., Robert de Comines).
- To prevent the area being used as a base for future rebellions.
- To give a warning about what could happen if you dared rebel against William.
- To destroy the motivation and spirit of the people of the north.

Features

- Took place in the winter of 1069/70 in Yorkshire and neighbouring shires.
- Homes burnt down, crops and seed destroyed, farm animals killed, people murdered.
- Salt was ploughed into the farmland so nothing would grow there.

Knowledge

5 Anglo-Saxon resistance

The impact of the Harrying of the North

Immediate impact

- An estimated 100 000 people died. Some were murdered by William's troops; others starved or froze to death. There were reports of cannibalism. Others took to eating cats and dogs.
- Without homes or useable farmland, thousands of people left the region as refugees.

Long-term impact

- The **Domesday Book** (a complete record of property ownership across England, written in 1086), records that 80 per cent of Yorkshire was known as 'waste', which means it was uncultivated and unpopulated.
- There were no further major Anglo-Saxon rebellions in the north.
- William began to replace the old Anglo-Saxon aristocracy with Norman followers. This tightened his grip on the country.

Changes in landownership

- At first, William allowed most Anglo-Saxons to keep their land, but split the large earldoms without an earl (e.g., if the earl had been killed at Hastings) into smaller areas and appointed Normans to govern them. These men were known as **barons** or **tenants-in-chief**. By 1076, only two earldoms were still held by Anglo-Saxons.
- William gradually replaced the 5 000 or so Anglo-Saxon thegns with Norman landowners, when thegns died or rebelled. The Domesday Book shows that, by 1086, there had been significant changes in landownership: most of the land was now controlled by Normans. Only 13 out of 1 000 tenants-in-chief were Anglo-Saxons.

How William I maintained royal power

William used a range of strategies to maintain his power.

1 Religion

William controlled who was appointed to the senior positions in the Church. This meant that the monarch could control some of the messages given out in churches.

2 Military strength

William maintained a large army and built hundreds of castles throughout England in towns, on borders, near key rivers, and in trouble spots (such as the Welsh Marches).

3 Terror

Whole villages were destroyed in the Harrying of the North. The Normans executed, imprisoned, or mutilated the rebels.

4 Land ownership

William confiscated land and titles from Anglo-Saxons to reward his followers. He could remove land if he felt someone was not loyal.

5 Royal visibility

William wanted his power and status to be visible to the whole country, to reinforce his role as king, and to maintain relations with key supporters. He travelled to different parts of England to visit important families and took part in ceremonies where he wore his crown. His image featured on coins and **writs** (letters from the king), which reinforced his role.

The Revolt of the Earls, 1075

The 1075 Revolt of the Earls involved three earls appointed by William: two Normans (Ralph de Gael, Earl of Norfolk, and Roger de Breteuil, Earl of Hereford) and the last surviving Anglo-Saxon earl (Waltheof, Earl of Northumbria).

There were three reasons for the revolt:

1 The earls were angry about loss of land, privileges, and power

For example, William and his sheriffs had been hearing legal cases in Roger's lands instead of Roger himself.

2 King Philip I of France encouraged Roger to rebel

Philip did not want Normandy to be more powerful than the rest of France, so he was eager to distract William's attention away from the area. Ralph and Roger were also promised other aid from overseas.

3 William was not in England

He had been in Normandy since 1073, leaving Archbishop Lanfranc in charge. William's absence gave the conspirators an ideal opportunity to rebel.

- Ralph, Roger, and Waltheof planned the revolt at the wedding feast of Ralph and Emma (Roger's sister). Lots of important earls and bishops were there. Waltheof had strong contacts with King Swegn of Denmark: the rebels expected his support for their plan.
- Waltheof then revealed the plan to Archbishop Lanfranc, who tried to persuade Roger not to rebel.
- Roger pressed ahead and Lanfranc sent men to find out what was going on.
- Roger's forces were stopped by the fyrd in Worcestershire and he was later imprisoned.
- Local troops were used to prevent Ralph from leaving Herefordshire: he eventually escaped to Brittany.
- The Danish army eventually arrived after the revolt had ended. They raided York then returned home. William returned after the Danes arrived.
- Waltheof initially escaped abroad but was tricked by William into returning and imprisoned, then beheaded.

Effects of the revolt

- William realised he needed to be careful of his own earls, who resented his power.
- Some Anglo-Saxons had joined the loyal Normans, suggesting that William had some Anglo-Saxon support.
- Waltheof's execution suggests that William was still prepared to come down hard on Anglo-Saxon rebellion.
- The failure of the Danish invasion in 1075 ended any major Viking threat to England.

Key terms Make sure you can write a definition for these key terms

geld tax Harrying of the North guerrilla barons tenants-in-chief Domesday Book writs

Retrieval

Learn the answers to the questions below, then cover the answers column with a piece of paper and write down as many as you can. Check and repeat.

Questions	Answers
1 Which two Anglo-Saxon earls led a rebellion in 1068?	Edwin and Morcar
2 Give two reasons why the 1068 rebellion took place.	Two from: William had not kept a promise he had made to Edwin that he could marry one of his daughters / Edwin's earldom and Morcar's earldom had been reduced in size / William had imposed heavy taxes, and had taken lots of Anglo-Saxon treasure / Norman castles were appearing all over the country
3 Name the Scottish king who was a powerful ally of Edgar Aethling.	King Malcolm III
4 Give two reasons why the Harrying of the North took place.	Two from: William was angry that the Anglo-Saxon leaders would not accept him as king / revenge for the deaths of Norman supporters / to prevent the area being used as a base for future rebellions / to give a warning about what could happen if you dared rebel / to destroy motivation and spirit of the people in the area
5 Identify one immediate impact of the Harrying of the North.	One from: homes burnt down, crops and seed destroyed, farm animals killed / without homes or useable farmland, thousands of people left the region as refugees / around 100 000 people died
6 Identify one long-term impact of the Harrying of the North.	One from: Domesday Book (1086) records that 80 per cent of Yorkshire was known as 'waste' (uncultivated and unpopulated) / no further major Anglo-Saxon rebellions in the north / William began to replace the old Anglo-Saxon aristocracy with Norman followers, which tightened his grip on the country
7 What was a 'tenant-in-chief'?	A man appointed to govern part of what had once been an Anglo-Saxon earldom
8 By 1076, how many Anglo-Saxon earls were there in England?	Only two
9 Why was William keen to travel to different parts of England and take part in ceremonies where he wore his crown?	He wanted his power and status to be visible to the whole country, to reinforce his role as king, and to maintain relations with key supporters
10 Which Anglo-Saxon earl took part in the Revolt of the Earls?	Earl of Northumbria, Waltheof

Put paper here

Previous questions

Use the questions below to check your knowledge from previous chapters.

Questions	Answers
1 When did Edward the Confessor die?	5 January 1066
2 What was a 'feigned retreat'?	A tactic where soldiers from one side pretend to retreat in the hope that enemy soldiers will follow and be in a vulnerable position
3 Why was William I so keen to control the Marches?	There were powerful Welsh princes in this area, which were a potential threat to William, especially if they joined with any English rebels

Put paper here

Practice

Exam-style questions

1 Describe **two** features of William of Normandy's claim to the English throne. **(4)**

2 Explain why William faced threats to his throne after 1066. **(12)**

> You **may** use the following in your answer:
> - Edgar Aethling
> - Hereward the Wake
>
> You **must** also use information of your own.

EXAM TIP

'Explain' means saying how or why something happened or why something was important. Always back up what you write with examples.

3 'The main reason William I was able to keep control of England in the years 1066–75 was because of the harsh punishments given to rebels.'

How far do you agree? Explain your answer. **(16)**

> You **may** use the following in your answer:
> - changes in land ownership
> - motte and bailey castles
>
> You **must** also use information of your own.

EXAM TIP

When writing your answer to the 16-mark question, aim to spend between 25 and 30 minutes on it. There is also an additional four marks in this question for your spelling, punctuation, and grammar, and use of specialist terms.

Knowledge

6 The feudal system and the Church

The Anglo-Saxon system of land ownership

Before the Norman invasion, England was divided into earldoms, governed by earls who could become incredibly powerful (Godwin, Earl of Wessex, is a good example).

The king could make anyone an earl and give them land to ensure their support. However, he was also free to take away land and could call upon his earls to provide an army in times of war.

The Norman system of land ownership

Feudalism is a system of give and take, based on control of the land (e.g., land in exchange for military service, tenancy in exchange for labour).

The system of give and take was very similar to what had existed in England before the Norman Conquest. However, a big change was that now William himself owned all the land in England.

- If any land-user did not provide the service or duty required of them, his land would be taken from him, a punishment known as **forfeiture**. It was a powerful way of controlling landowners.
- When a landholder died, the heir did not automatically inherit the land. First, they had to swear loyalty to William and pay a fee (as much as William thought they could afford).
- Everyone knew their position in the **feudal system**: what was expected of them, and what they needed to do for the people above and below them in the hierarchy.

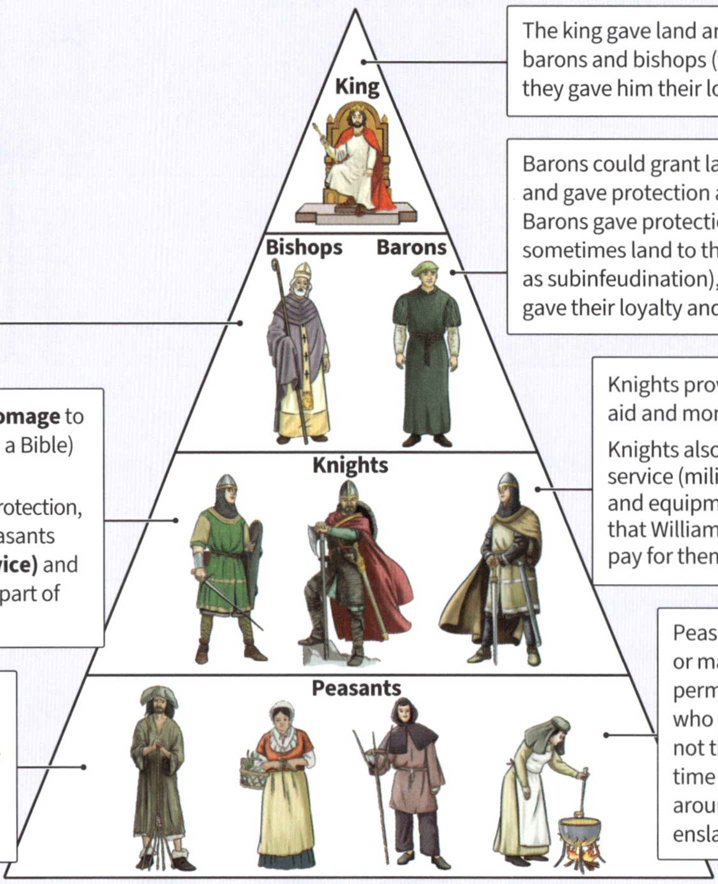

The king gave land and titles (known as a fief) to his barons and bishops (tenants-in-chief) and in return they gave him their loyalty and military service.

Barons could grant land through **subinfeudation** and gave protection and justice.
Barons gave protection, shelter, food, and sometimes land to their knights (a process known as subinfeudination), and in return the knights gave their loyalty and military service.

25 per cent of land was controlled by the Church.

Knights provided **knight service** (military aid and money) and loyalty to the king.

Knights also had to provide unpaid knight service (military help, money, weapons, and equipment) to the king. This ensured that William had troops without having to pay for them himself.

All landholders had to **pay homage** to William: a promise (sworn on a Bible) to stay loyal.
Knights gave peasants food, protection, and shelter, and in return peasants worked in fields **(labour service)** and gave their military service as part of the fyrd.

Peasants could not leave the land or marry without the lord's permission; some were 'freemen' who paid rent to the lord but were not tied to him in other ways. At the time of the Norman Conquest, around ten per cent of people were enslaved. William banned slavery.

Provided labour service for the lord in return for protection and the use of the lord's land. It involved farm work or providing food and crops.

▲ *The feudal system*

How far did the Norman Conquest transform England?

The Normans did change life in England. However, the extent of change differed according to social status. For the **aristocracy** at the top of the hierarchy when the Normans arrived, the impact was significant, with an almost complete change from the Anglo-Saxon system. However, for the peasants at the bottom of the social scale, there was little change.

King William's intention was not to change every aspect of English life and make it Norman. Instead, he took aspects from both systems to make sure that the governments of England and Normandy were successful, efficient, profitable and, most importantly, secure.

Land

Aristocracy

- Initially William tried to keep Anglo-Saxon landowners in place, but many took part in rebellions and he replaced them with Normans whom he could trust.
- Before the invasion, a few earls controlled most of the land. William divided the land into much smaller areas (fiefs), which made the new landowners less powerful.
- A new group, known as knights, were also able to hold land.

Peasants

- Life for peasants changed very little. Farm life went on as before – they just had a new person to work for.

Military

Aristocracy

- Castles were built to establish status and protect the new landowners from the local Anglo-Saxon population.
- Over time, castles became centres of trade and commerce.

Peasants

- The size of castles, and the speed at which they were built, would no doubt have intimidated the local population.
- Land was seized and cleared for the castles.
- Many locals, such as the blacksmith, worked within the walls of the bailey and so were protected from attack.

Government and law

Aristocracy

- William kept most of the Anglo-Saxon financial system.
- Trial by jury was introduced, but only the Norman aristocracy had the right to demand it.
- Anglo-Saxons were gradually removed from positions of power and influence.

Peasants

- New forest laws meant that peasants could no longer hunt to supplement their diets.
- Everyone living in the fief was required to pay towards a fine for any attack on a Norman.

Trade

Aristocracy

- William stopped trade with Viking countries. This especially impacted the north. Trade with Normandy increased, which boosted the south of England.
- The Normans brought stability in trade and this led to the development of many towns. Between 1066 and 1100, 21 new towns were created around the country.

Peasants

- Towns kept their trading rights and privileges.
- Many were able to specialise in a particular product or material.

Key terms Make sure you can write a definition for these key terms

feudalism forfeiture feudal system subinfeudation pay homage labour service knight service aristocracy

Knowledge

6 The feudal system and the Church

The role of the Church under the Normans

The Normans practised Christianity, like the Anglo-Saxons before them. The Church was central to everyday life and had a huge influence on society.

The role of the Church under the Normans

Symbolism
Large churches, vast cathedrals (such as Durham), abbeys, and monasteries were built to show devotion to God. They were also built to dominate the landscape, as castles did, and to show the English that the Normans were now in charge.

Priests
Priests were central figures. They led daily services, took confession, and helped the sick. Everyone went to the priest for advice, from peasants to the lord of the manor.

Economics
- The Church was a major landowner and peasants were required to work on its land for free (if they didn't, they believed God would punish them).
- **Tithes** (a tax of 10 per cent) were collected on everything that a farm produced.

Pilgrimage
An important part of people's lives. The wealthy journeyed to Jerusalem: others visited holy sites such as monasteries and abbeys in England.

Education
The Church produced all books, which meant that it controlled which books were published. Books were copied out by monks.

Law
The Church heard court cases for crimes committed on its land.

Politics
Leading **clergy** advised the king on national matters.

Religion
- The Church's main role was to teach people to live a good life and so go to heaven.
- Most people could not read; they learned about heaven and hell from sermons and paintings on church walls.

Health
- Disease was widely seen as a punishment from God.
- People turned to the Church for help when they were sick – priests might suggest they ask God for forgiveness through prayer or by giving money to the Church.

William I and the Church

When William invaded England, he did so under the Papal Banner and in the belief that God was on his side. Once he was king, he set about dealing with what he saw as four major corruptions in the English Church: pluralism, simony, nepotism, and marriage.

When William became king, Stigand was the Archbishop of Canterbury. Stigand had been appointed because he was a close ally of Earl Godwin. However, Stigand was accused of allowing the corruption in the Church to happen. In 1070, William replaced Stigand as archbishop with his choice.

Pluralism	Clergy holding and being paid for multiple jobs, and sometimes doing none of them.
Simony	Selling positions or jobs within the Church.
Nepotism	Appointing unqualified family members to positions of power.
Marriage	In Normandy, clergy were required to remain celibate (no sex). In England, many priests were married and had children.

Lanfranc's reforms of the Church

Lanfranc was a strict leader and brought in many reforms. Lanfranc and William 'Normanised' the Church, which meant that the reforms reflected the ideas, beliefs, and practices of the Normans.

Area	Reform
Bishops	• By 1080, there was only one Anglo-Saxon bishop left. William had replaced the others with Normans.
Architecture	• Churches and cathedrals were rebuilt in the Norman style, with its simple yet impressive design. • More monasteries were built – places dedicated to a spiritual life.
Organisation	• The Church was given a clear structure. Dioceses (districts overseen by bishops) were divided into archdeaconries (archdeacons), which were divided into deaneries (deans), which were divided into parishes (parish priests). • New cathedrals were built in important locations such as Coventry, Salisbury, and Lincoln.
Legal issues	• From 1076, clergy were not tried in everyday courts. Only special Church courts could try clergy. • The number of archdeacons was increased. They enforced Church discipline.
Parish priests	• Lanfranc wanted priests to live spiritual lives, so he banned marriage and made celibacy compulsory for priests. However, most Anglo-Saxon parish priests remained in their jobs and, despite attempts at reform, many remained married.

Impact of Church reforms on William's power

- New bishops paid homage to the king. Church land could be forfeited if William wanted.
- When a bishop or archbishop died, William chose his successor.
- Parish priests had to follow Norman procedures. William controlled communication between the Pope, church leaders, and people. As the Church influenced every aspect of people's lives, this meant that William shaped the messages people heard about the king and God.

Key terms **Make sure you can write a definition for these key terms**

tithes clergy pluralism simony nepotism

Retrieval

Learn the answers to the questions below, then cover the answers column with a piece of paper and write down as many as you can. Check and repeat.

	Questions	Answers
1	Define the 'feudal system'.	A system of give and take, with the king at the top and all others in society in order of status and importance below
2	Which group were at the bottom of the feudal system?	Peasants
3	If any land-user in the system did not provide the service or duty required of them, William could take the land away from them. What was this punishment called?	Forfeiture
4	What was 'labour service'?	The work a peasant did in return for protection and the use of the lord's land, involving farm work or providing food and crops
5	What would a knight be required to do as part of their 'knight service'?	A knight had to provide unpaid military help, money, weapons, and equipment for the king
6	What was the name of the ten per cent tax payment collected on everything that a farm produced?	Tithe
7	By 1080, how many Anglo-Saxon bishops were there?	One
8	What laws prevented peasants from hunting in woodlands and forests?	Forest laws
9	William stopped trade with which area of Europe?	Viking countries
10	Between 1066 and 1100, how many new towns were cre ated around the country?	21
11	What was a 'pilgrimage'?	A journey to Jerusalem in the Holy Land, or another holy site such as a monastery or abbey in England
12	Give two examples of what William felt was corrupt about the Church in England when he became king.	Two from: pluralism (clergy holding multiple jobs) / simony (selling Church positions) / nepotism (appointing family members) / priests marrying (in Normandy they were required to remain celibate)
13	Who was Archbishop of Canterbury when William became King of England?	Stigand
14	Who became Archbishop of Canterbury in 1070?	Lanfranc
15	William and Lanfranc 'Normanised' the Church in England. What is meant by this term?	The Church was changed to reflect the ideas, beliefs, and practices of the Normans

Put paper here

Previous questions

Use the questions below to check your knowledge from previous chapters.

Questions	Answers
1 Why did William's men believe they had God on their side?	They were fighting under the Papal Banner
2 Name the three new Marcher earldoms.	Chester, Shrewsbury, and Hereford
3 Which Anglo-Saxon earl took part in the Revolt of the Earls?	Earl of Northumbria, Waltheof

Put paper here

Practice

Exam-style questions

1 Describe **two** features of feudalism. **(4)**

> **EXAM TIP**
> Remember, you need to identify **two** valid features and write a sentence or two to support each feature. Don't spend a long time on this question, perhaps just five minutes.

2 Explain why William the Conqueror's methods of maintaining power helped him secure his position as King of England. **(12)**

You **may** use the following in your answer:
- rewarding followers
- Harrying of the North

You **must** also use information of your own.

> **EXAM TIP**
> This question is linked to the content on several pages of this revision guide. It will test your ability to think about the things you have learnt as a whole. For example, the revision work on the Harrying of the North is on pages 21 and 22 of this book, and lots of the information on the way William rewarded followers is in Chapters 4 and 5.

3 'The main consequence of the Norman invasion of England was the Normanisation of the Church.'

How far do you agree? Explain your answer. **(16)**

You **may** use the following in your answer:
- Archbishop Lanfranc
- the feudal system

You **must** also use information of your own.

Knowledge

7 Norman government

Centralised power

Under the Anglo-Saxons, no single person was in charge. The earls held power in their own earldoms.

Under the Normans, William I was at the centre of all decision-making and government. This is often called a system of '**centralised power**'.

Ways power was centred on William

- Decision-making was done where William was staying. There was no separate parliament building where people met away from the king to discuss things.
- All landowners swore an oath of loyalty to William.
- William was at the top of the feudal system.
- The Church was 'Normanised' on William's orders. He appointed people to all the major Church roles.
- William kept vast areas of land for himself (the '**royal demesne**').
- He used land to reward loyal followers, but retained the right to take it away from them too.
- William earned vast amounts of money by taxing land and religious places. The ten most powerful barons did not have as much wealth as William.
- The areas of land (fiefs) held by barons were not as large as those that had been held by Anglo-Saxon earls, so no single person had the power to seriously challenge him.

The role of regents

At the beginning of his reign, William spent a lot of time in England dealing with rebellions.

However, from 1072 until his death in 1087, he spent around three-quarters of his time back in Normandy. Whilst away, he left a regent in charge. **Regents** were trusted people who had the same power as the king did.

William's regents were:

- Odo of Bayeux, his half-brother
- William FitzOsbern, his long-time friend
- Lanfranc, Archbishop of Canterbury.

The role of sheriffs

Anglo-Saxon kings used a shire reeve (sheriff) to run each shire. They collected taxes and fines, held courts to deal with major crimes, and raised an army if needed.

The sheriff's role stayed mostly the same when William became king. However, he replaced Anglo-Saxons with Normans and the Norman sheriffs had a lot more power. For example:

- Norman sheriffs answered only to the king. As a result, they were a symbol of Norman power and control.
- They were entitled to a share of the tax they collected. This meant they could make themselves very rich and meant some sheriffs taxed the local people heavily.
- They seized a lot of land for themselves and became major landowners. Because of their power, people had nobody to complain to.

The introduction of the 'forest'

William was a keen hunter, and extended the area in which he hunted by taking land away from landowners.

The land became William's 'royal demesne' and was classed as 'forest'. This didn't necessarily mean it was a wooded area; a 'forest' was any land that William wanted to use for hunting, including farmland.

Entire areas were turned into forest, such as the New Forest in southern England.

1. 'Forest' areas had their own strict rules, and there were harsh punishments if the 'forest laws' were broken.
2. The quarry (animals that were hunted) was protected.
3. Damage to any vegetation needed by the quarry was banned.
4. Only the king and people he gave permission to were allowed to bring hunting weapons and hunting dogs into the forest.
5. There were strict restrictions on cutting wood, building homes, and clearing land in the forest.

The significance of the 'forest'

- It showed that the king was in absolute control – he could take what land he wanted. The forests were a hated symbol of power for ordinary people.
- By grabbing so much land himself, William made any land-grabbing done by sheriffs and barons look more acceptable.
- The harsh punishments for breaking forest laws, which showed how brutal Norman rule could be.
- William earned vast sums of money from the forests, from the sale of hunting rights and from fines for breaking forest laws.

The Domesday Book

The Domesday Survey (which later became the Domesday Book) was carried out in 1086. It is the biggest gathering of information in English history and has become an invaluable source of evidence for historians.

There are a number of theories as to why William I ordered the Domesday Survey. Some of the main reasons considered are:

- to help collect taxes accurately and so ensure that William got as much money as possible
- to make sure barons were not hiding wealth that could be used to threaten his position
- to record and settle arguments over land that existed after the invasion
- to make it clear that all land was held by permission of the king and that in return landholders owed him loyalty and military service.

What does the Domesday Book tell us?

- It tells us who owned the land and where they owned it, and how much that land and property was worth.
- It tells us how many Norman settlers (10 000) and knights (2 000) there were in total. The total population of England was between 1.5 and 2 million people.
- It tells us what taxes were owed from the time of Edward the Confessor, showing how landowners changed from Anglo-Saxons under Edward the Confessor to Normans under William I.

Key terms Make sure you can write a definition for these key terms

centralised power   royal demesne   regents

Retrieval

Learn the answers to the questions below, then cover the answers column with a piece of paper and write down as many as you can. Check and repeat.

	Questions	Answers
1	What is meant when we say that William was at the 'centre of government'?	All decision-making and government was centred around the king. He controlled all elements of governing the country
2	What term is used to describe the land that William kept directly for himself?	Royal demesne
3	From 1072 until his death in 1087, about how much time did William spend in Normandy?	Three-quarters
4	What was a 'regent'?	A trusted person in charge of England whilst the king was away
5	Name two regents of England during William's reign.	Two from: William used Odo of Bayeux, William FitzOsbern, and Lanfranc as regents
6	List two of the roles of an Anglo-Saxon sheriff.	Two from: they collected taxes and fines / carried out justice (in 'shire courts') for major crimes / raised an army if needed
7	Give two reasons why Norman sheriffs were resented.	Two from: the Norman sheriffs had more power and answered only to the king, so they were viewed as a symbol of Norman power and control / they often taxed the local people heavily / they seized a lot of land for themselves / people had nobody to complain to.
8	Define what William regarded as a 'forest'.	A 'forest' was any area of land that William wanted to use for hunting – and this might include farmland
9	List two laws that applied in the forest.	Two from: quarry was protected / damage to any vegetation used by the quarry was banned / hunting weapons and hunting dogs banned / strict restrictions on cutting wood, building homes, and clearing land
10	When was the Domesday Survey carried out?	1086
11	Give two theories why the Domesday Survey was carried out.	Two from: to help collect taxes accurately and so ensure that William got as much money as possible / to make sure barons were not hiding wealth / to record and settle arguments over land / to make it clear that all land was held by permission of the king in return for loyalty
12	According to the survey, what was the approximate population of England in 1086?	Between 1.5 and 2 million people

Put paper here

Previous questions

Use the questions below to check your knowledge from previous chapters.

Questions		Answers
1	Which two Anglo-Saxon earls led a rebellion in 1068?	Edwin and Morcar
2	What would a knight be required to do as part of their 'knight service'?	A knight had to provide unpaid military help, money, weapons, and equipment for the king
3	Who became Archbishop of Canterbury in 1070?	Lanfranc

Put paper here

Practice

Exam-style questions

1 Describe **two** features of the Domesday Book. **(4)**

2 Explain why changes in land ownership made resistance to William I's control less likely. **(12)**

> You **may** use the following in your answer:
> - tenants-in-chief
> - centralised power
>
> You **must** also use information of your own.

EXAM TIP

Notice that tenants-in-chief are mentioned in questions 2 and 3. You need to be able to manipulate what you know and apply it to the specific question. In this case, you need to know all about tenants-in-chief, but are required to apply the knowledge differently in each question.

3 'It was changes in land ownership that did the most to secure Norman control of England.'

How far do you agree? Explain your answer. **(16)**

> You **may** use the following in your answer:
> - tenants-in-chief
> - motte and bailey castles
>
> You **must** also use information of your own.

EXAM TIP

Notice that this question gets you thinking right back to the work you did towards the start of the topic when you looked at the reasons for the building of castles, their key features, and importance.

Knowledge

8 The Norman aristocracy

Who were the Norman aristocracy?

The Norman aristocracy were the small, privileged ruling class of wealthy, powerful people who controlled the land in Norman England.

The culture and language of the Norman aristocracy gradually replaced Anglo-Saxon language and culture.

What languages were spoken in Norman England?

Three main languages were spoken in Norman England:

French	Latin	English
The language of the new Norman aristocracy. Also used in court, in law, and in government.	Used for official documents and religious services (as in most of Western Europe).	Continued to be used by peasants. In time, some Norman words were used in everyday speech.

As time went on, English and Norman-French began to merge to create Anglo-Norman.

Norman culture

Many different things make up a group's culture, for example, food, language, clothing, music, art, customs, and religion. The new Norman aristocracy's culture became more high status than Anglo-Saxon culture, and began to dominate in the upper levels of society.

Norman culture

- Building large castles, cathedrals, and abbeys was another way to show off status, and devotion to God. Many Anglo-Saxon churches were knocked down and replaced by Norman ones in the **Romanesque** style (with clean lines, rounded arches, and vaulted ceilings).
- The Norman aristocracy liked to show off their wealth with expensive fabrics and furs.
- Hunting was a popular pastime, as well as feasting and dancing. A group of acrobats or jugglers might entertain a baron and his guests.
- Falconry (also known as 'hawking') was also very popular for both men and women. Specially trained birds of prey would fly and catch smaller animals.
- It was common in Anglo-Saxon England to divide up land among the family when someone died. The Normans established the idea of **primogeniture**, where the first-born son inherits everything.
- The Normans were religious and believed they should atone for the violent conquest of England. This often meant building churches and cathedrals, and giving money to the Church. The Normans followed a moral code known as **chivalry**, inspired by Christian teachings. Chivalry demanded that they were truthful, loyal, and brave in battle – and fair even to their enemies.

Key terms Make sure you can write a definition for these key terms

Romanesque primogeniture chivalry

The career and significance of Bishop Odo

Date	Event	Significance
c1036	Odo is born. He is William I's half-brother; they shared the same mother, Herleva.	
c1049	William appoints Odo Bishop of Bayeux, one of the most important towns in Normandy.	Shows that William trusted Odo. He wanted a reliable family member in an influential position in this key town.
1066	Odo helps organise the invasion of England and contributes 100 ships to the invasion fleet. Odo fights at the Battle of Hastings and is rewarded with lots of land (only William I has more land in England than Odo).	Odo became a powerful landowner but he was resented by the Anglo-Saxons who lost the land William I gave to him.
1067	Appointed Earl of Kent (a vital area on the southeast coast that needed defending). Odo and William FitzOsbern left as regents when William returns to Normandy.	Again, shows how much William trusted Odo. Odo was brutal with the Anglo-Saxons and they hated him. He acted cruelly and illegally seized land. It was a disaster for relations between the Anglo-Saxons and William I, who did not want to provoke Anglo-Saxon rebellions.
c1070	The Bayeux Tapestry is commissioned by, it is believed, Odo (he features in it several times).	The Bayeux Tapestry was a piece of Norman propaganda, designed to show that William I was the rightful king of England.
1075	Odo leads an army against the Earl of Norfolk and ends the Revolt of the Earls.	
1076	Odo is put on trial following a dispute with Archbishop Lanfranc. He is accused of illegally seizing land and property and is forced to return it.	Shows the power and influence of Lanfranc. Also, that there were limits to what the Norman aristocracy could do: William respected the law above a family member.
1080	The Norman Bishop of Durham is murdered by English rebels. William I sends Odo to deal with them.	Shows that Odo was viewed as a skilled military leader.
1082	Odo is arrested and imprisoned for misconduct (he may have taken Church funds or attempted to travel to Italy to become Pope). William I imprisons Odo in Normandy.	Shows that William I would not accept challenges to his power and authority, even from close family members.
1087	On his deathbed, William I agrees to release Odo from prison.	
1088	Odo rebels against William I's son and successor, William Rufus. The rebellion fails. William II banishes Odo from England and takes his land.	
1097	Odo joins the First Crusade in 1095 and dies on his way to Jerusalem.	

REVISION TIP

Prepare short 'fact files' on some of the topic's 'big names', such as William I, King Harold, Edward the Confessor, Odo, Lanfranc, Morcar, and FitzOsbern. Familiarity with the roles people played can help you make better sense of events.

Retrieval

Learn the answers to the questions below, then cover the answers column with a piece of paper and write down as many as you can. Check and repeat.

	Questions	Answers
1	Define what is meant by the term 'Norman aristocracy'.	The small, privileged ruling class of wealthy, powerful people who controlled the land in Norman England
2	What language was spoken by the new Norman aristocracy?	French
3	What language was used for official documents and religious services?	Latin
4	List three examples of what makes up a group's 'culture'.	Three from: food / language / clothing / music / art / customs / religion
5	Give one reason why the Normans built large cathedrals, abbeys, and castles.	One from: to show off wealth and status / to show devotion to God
6	What architectural style, named after the Roman style with clean lines, rounded arches and vaulted ceilings, was popular in Norman building?	Romanesque
7	List three games or leisure activities enjoyed by the Norman aristocracy.	Three from: hunting / feasting / dancing / watching acrobats or jugglers / playing chess, draughts, cards, or throwing dice / falconry ('hawking')
8	In what way did the Normans change the rules of inheritance?	It was common in Anglo-Saxon England to divide up land among the family when someone died. The Normans established the idea of primogeniture, where the first-born son inherits everything
9	Define 'chivalry'.	A moral code inspired by Christian teachings, demanding honesty, loyalty, and bravery in battle, treating enemies fairly, and never breaking a promise
10	What relation was Odo to William I?	He was William's half-brother (they shared the same mother, Herleva)
11	How was Odo involved in the invasion of England?	Odo helped organise the invasion, contributed 100 ships to the invasion fleet, fought in the battle of Hastings, and was rewarded with lots of land
12	What did Odo commission in 1070?	The Bayeux Tapestry
13	In what year was Odo put on trial following a dispute with Archbishop Lanfranc?	1076
14	Why was Odo arrested and imprisoned in 1082?	For misconduct (he may have taken Church funds or made an attempt to travel to Italy to become Pope)
15	What happened to Odo from 1088 to his death in 1097?	In 1088, Odo rebelled against William I's son and successor, William Rufus. The rebellion failed and William II banished Odo from England and took his land. Odo joined the First Crusade in 1095 and died on his way to Jerusalem in 1097

Put paper here

Previous questions

Use the questions below to check your knowledge from previous chapters.

	Questions	Answers
1	Why did William secure the trading ports in Kent?	To stop Anglo-Saxon trade and allow supplies to be brought in from Normandy
2	Who was Archbishop of Canterbury when William became King of England?	Stigand
3	Name two regents of England during William's reign.	Two from: William used Odo of Bayeux, William FitzOsbern, and Lanfranc as regents

Put paper here

Practice

Exam-style questions

1 Describe **two** features of the culture of Norman aristocracy. **(4)**

EXAM TIP

One of the biggest problems with 'describe' questions is that students often write too much. Make sure you stick to the question – simply describe two features of the culture of the Norman aristocracy.

2 Explain why Odo was important in Norman England in the years 1066–88. **(12)**

You **may** use the following in your answer:

- Battle of Hastings
- regent

You **must** also use information of your own.

EXAM TIP

It is important to decode the question carefully. This particular question focuses on the importance of Bishop Odo. It is not asking you about the importance of the Battle of Hastings or the importance of regents in general. It is asking about Bishop Odo specifically, and is simply giving you the bullet points to inspire you.

3 'The main reason William I was able to keep control of the people of England was his use of regents.'

How far do you agree? Explain your answer. **(16)**

You **may** use the following in your answer:

- regents
- sheriffs

You **must** also use information of your own.

Knowledge

9 William I and his sons

William I's character

William I's character

Very religious
Promoted Church reform and encouraged the building of churches, cathedrals, abbeys, and monasteries.

Devoted husband
William and his wife Matilda had nine children.

Ruthless and cruel
Put down rebellions very harshly and even imprisoned his half-brother, Odo.

Loved wealth
Wore fine clothes and lots of jewellery, and tried to squeeze as much money out of people as he could.

Tough, expert fighter
Survived several assassination attempts when he was young in Normandy, and was a skilled military leader.

Politically smart
Managed to remain king until his death in 1087 (as well as being Duke of Normandy).

William I's son Robert and revolt in Normandy (1077–80)

William I had three sons: Robert (the eldest), William Rufus, and Henry.

Robert had a poor relationship with both his father and his younger brother William Rufus. Robert was bullied by his father. He was given the mocking nickname Robert Curthose ('short stockings'/ 'dumpy legs').

William I felt that Robert was lazy and spoiled. When William was in England, he trusted his wife, Matilda, to rule Normandy, rather than Robert.

1077

Robert brawled with his two younger brothers when a prank involving urine went wrong. Robert, enraged, felt his brothers weren't punished enough, and the next day tried to take control of Rouen Castle in Normandy. He failed, but he had the support of William's enemy, the King of France, who gave Robert a castle at Gerberoy as a base from which to launch attacks against Normandy.

1079

William I attacked the castle at Gerberoy but was defeated (and was injured during the fighting). Also, unknown to William I, Matilda was sending money to Robert in support of her son. This was all very humiliating for William.

1080

Matilda organised a peace settlement between William I and Robert. William I made Robert his heir in Normandy.

William I's death (1087)

William I was injured in July 1087 whilst out riding in France. He suffered in pain for weeks before he died on 9 September.

In the hope of avoiding conflict after his death, and because he did not believe Robert had the ability to govern the whole country, William I declared that the inheritance would be split as follows:

- Robert would have Normandy
- William Rufus would rule England
- Henry would receive the substantial sum of £5000.

This went against the Norman tradition of primogeniture and Robert was unhappy with it. He believed that as the eldest son he should rule both Normandy and England.

William I sent William Rufus to England with a letter for Lanfranc instructing the archbishop to arrange for William Rufus to be crowned King of England. Lanfranc crowned William Rufus as King William II in September 1087.

Odo and Robert's rebellion (1088)

Norman landowners, who had land in both Normandy and England, wanted the two places to be united under one ruler. They had promised to be loyal to both William II (as King of England) and Robert (as Duke of Normandy). Therefore, if these two men fought each other, the landowners would be in a difficult position!

By now, Bishop Odo had been released from prison. He said that landowners should choose between Robert of Normandy and William II as their united leader. Odo wanted Robert as the united leader because he felt he would be easier to control than William Rufus (who was more like his father than Robert).

In 1088, Odo led a rebellion against William II, in support of Robert. There were some outbreaks of rebellion in England in support of Odo and Robert, causing a serious threat to William II. However, Odo did not get the support from other Norman aristocrats, the English bishops, or the general population.

↓

Odo (and his brother, Robert of Mortain) took refuge in Pevensey Castle (near Hastings). They held out for several weeks but were eventually defeated.

↓

Odo managed to escape to Rochester Castle in Kent, and awaited the help of Robert. Robert never came to help Odo, the rebellions faded away, and Odo was exiled.

↓

William II secured his throne and his popularity by promising to lower taxes and get rid of the hated forest laws. However, he soon went back on these promises.

Retrieval

Learn the answers to the questions below, then cover the answers column with a piece of paper and write down as many as you can. Check and repeat.

Questions	Answers
1 List three aspects of William I's character.	Three from: devoted husband / very religious / ruthless and cruel / tough, expert fighter / politically smart / loved wealth
2 What was the name of William I's wife?	Matilda
3 What were the first names of King William's three surviving sons?	Robert, William Rufus, and Henry
4 Which of King William's three sons was nicknamed 'Curthose'?	Robert
5 Describe the relationship between King William and his eldest son.	Robert had a poor relationship with his father. Robert was bullied by his father. William felt that Robert was lazy and spoiled. He trusted his wife, Matilda, to rule Normandy, rather than Robert
6 After Robert rebelled against his father from 1077, when was peace eventually restored and Robert made William's heir in Normandy?	1080
7 When did William I die?	9 September 1087
8 Describe how William I decided to organise the inheritance of England and Normandy after his death.	William declared that the inheritance would be split: Robert would have Normandy, William Rufus would rule England, and Henry would receive the substantial sum of £5000
9 In what way did the way William I organised his legacy break the Norman tradition of inheritance?	He went against the Norman tradition of primogeniture: as the eldest son, Robert should have inherited and ruled both Normandy and England
10 Who crowned William Rufus as King of England?	Archbishop Lanfranc
11 When was William II crowned?	September 1087
12 Why did Norman landowners want both England and Normandy to be ruled by the same person?	They had promised to be loyal to both William II (as King of England) and Robert (as Duke of Normandy). If these two men fought each other, the landowners would be in a difficult position
13 Why did Bishop Odo want Robert Curthose as the united leader of both England and Normandy?	Odo wanted Robert as the united leader because he felt he would be easier to control than William Rufus (who was more like his father than Robert)
14 Who did not support Odo in the rebellion against William II?	Other Norman aristocrats, the English bishops, and the general population. Also, Robert himself did not help Odo

Put paper here

Previous questions

Use the questions below to check your knowledge from previous chapters.

Questions		Answers
1	Name the Scottish king who was a powerful ally of Edgar Aethling.	King Malcolm III
2	What was 'labour service'?	The work a peasant did in return for protection and the use of the lord's land, involving farm work or providing food and crops
3	Define what is meant by the term 'Norman aristocracy'.	The small, privileged ruling class of wealthy, powerful people who controlled the land in Norman England

Put paper here

Practice

Exam-style questions

1 Describe **two** features of the career of Bishop Odo. **(4)**

2 Explain why Robert of Normandy rebelled against his father in 1077–80. **(12)**

You **may** use the following in your answer:

- Robert's brothers
- William I

You **must** also use information of your own.

EXAM TIP

Make sure you know the question types you will be asked in each part of the examination. Find out how many marks there are for each type of question.

3 'The main consequence of William I's decisions about the succession was that William Rufus inherited the English crown.'

How far do you agree? Explain your answer. **(16)**

You **may** use the following in your answer:

- Robert of Normandy
- Bishop Odo

You **must** also use information of your own.

EXAM TIP

Your conclusion is a crucial part of your answer. You have been asked what you think about the statement and so you must state clearly how far you agree with it and your reasons why you think what you think.

OXFORD
UNIVERSITY PRESS

Great Clarendon Street, Oxford, OX2 6DP, United Kingdom

Oxford University Press is a department of the University of Oxford. It furthers the University's objective of excellence in research, scholarship, and education by publishing worldwide. Oxford is a registered trade mark of Oxford University Press in the UK and in certain other countries.

Written by Aaron Wilkes

Series Editor: Aaron Wilkes

The moral rights of the author have been asserted

First published in 2023

British Library Cataloguing in Publication Data
Data available

978-1-382-04300-7

10 9 8 7 6 5 4 3 2 1

The manufacturing process conforms to the environmental regulations of the country of origin.

Printed in the UK by Bell and Bain Ltd, Glasgow

Acknowledgements
The publisher and authors would like to thank the following for permission to use photographs and other copyright material:

Photos: piv: GRANGER - Historical Picture Archive / Alamy Stock Photo; **p7:** GRANGER - Historical Picture Archive / Alamy Stock Photo.

Artwork by Newgen Publishing, Aptara, Aptara / Newgen Publishing, Q2A Media, and Moreno Chiacchiera, Rudolf Farkas, Martin Sanders and Q2A Media.

Every effort has been made to contact copyright holders of material reproduced in this book. Any omissions will be rectified in subsequent printings if notice is given to the publisher.

Although we have made every effort to trace and contact all copyright holders before publication this has not been possible in all cases. If notified, the publisher will rectify any errors or omissions at the earliest opportunity.

Links to third party websites are provided by Oxford in good faith and for information only. Oxford disclaims any responsibility for the materials contained in any third party website referenced in this work.

FSC www.fsc.org MIX Paper | Supporting responsible forestry FSC® C007785